WINSTON

CHURCHILL

A LIFE IN 365 QUOTES

GREAT WORDS OF WIT AND WISDOM FROM HIS EARLY YEARS TO BRITAIN'S DARKEST HOUR AND BEYOND

ABSTRACT PRESS

ABSTRACT PRESS

First published in this edition 2021

ISBN-13: 9798733437323

WINSTON CHURCHILL

A LIFE IN 365 QUOTES

GREAT WORDS OF WIT AND WISDOM FROM HIS EARLY YEARS TO BRITAIN'S DARKEST HOUR AND BEYOND

1

Victory at all costs, victory in spite of all terror, victory however long and hard the road may be; for without victory, there is no survival.

2

I would say to the House, as I said to those who have joined this Government: 'I have nothing to offer but blood, toil, tears, and sweat.' We have before us an ordeal of the most grievous kind. We have before us many, many long months of struggle and of suffering. You ask, what is our policy? I will say: It is to wage war, by sea, land and air, with all our might and with all the strength that God can give us: to wage war against a monstrous tyranny, never surpassed in the dark, lamentable catalogue of human crime. That is our policy. You ask, what is our aim? I can answer in one word: It is victory, victory at all costs, victory in spite of all terror, victory, however long and hard the road may be; for without victory, there is no survival.

3

Perhaps it is better to be irresponsible and right, than to be responsible and wrong.

4

A state of society where men may not speak their minds cannot long endure.

5

If the human race wishes to have a prolonged and indefinite period of material prosperity, they have only got to behave in a peaceful and helpful way toward one another.

6

Sure I am of this, that you have only to endure to conquer. You have only to persevere to save yourselves, and to save all those who rely upon you. You have only to go right on, and at the end of the road, be it short or long, victory and honor will be found.

7

When you have to kill a man, it costs nothing to be polite.

8

It will not benefit the world if we succeed in banishing the old-fashioned wars of nations only to clear the board for social and doctrinal wars of even greater ferocity and destructiveness. This, indeed, is a growing danger. We were told that the old wars of religion had ended, but that is not much comfort if the wars of various kinds of secular religions or non-God religions are to begin and are to make Europe the arena of their hideous conflict, and if all that makes life worth living to the mass of the people is to be destroyed in the process.

9

Out of intense complexities intense simplicities emerge.

10

The farther backward you can look, the farther forward you can see.

11

War is mainly a catalogue of blunders.

12

When I look back on all these worries I remember the story of the old man who said on his deathbed that he had had a lot of trouble in his life, most of which had never happened.

13

Courage is what it takes to stand up and speak, it's also what it takes to sit down and listen.

14

Headmasters have powers at their disposal with which Prime Ministers have never yet been invested.

15

The British nation is unique in this respect. They are the only people who like to be told how bad things are, who like to be told the worst.

16

We shall not flag or fail. We shall go on to the end, we shall fight in France, we shall fight on the seas and oceans, we shall fight with growing confidence and growing strength in the air, we shall defend our Island, whatever the cost may be, we shall fight on the beaches, we shall fight on the landing grounds, we shall fight in the fields and in the streets, we shall fight in the hills; we shall never surrender, and even if, which I do not for a moment believe, this Island or a large part of it were subjugated and starving, then our Empire beyond the seas, armed and guarded by the British Fleet, would carry on the struggle, until, in God's good time, the New World, with all its power and might, steps forth to the rescue and the liberation of the Old.

17

Everything tends towards catastrophe and collapse. I am interested, geared up and happy. Is it not horrible to be made like this?

18

'No comment' is a splendid expression. I am using it again and again.

19

I am prepared to meet my Maker. Whether my Maker is prepared for the great ordeal of meeting me is another matter.

20

I never worry about action, but only inaction.

21

Christmas is a season not only of rejoicing but of reflection.

22

The gratitude of every home in our Island, in our Empire, and indeed throughout the world, except in the abodes of the guilty, goes out to the British airmen who, undaunted by odds, unwearied in their constant challenge and mortal danger, are turning the tide of the World War by their prowess and by their devotion. Never in the field of human conflict was so much owed by so many to so few. All hearts go out to the fighter pilots, whose brilliant actions we see with our own eyes day after day; but we must never forget that all the time, night after night, month after month, our bomber squadrons travel far into Germany, find their targets in the darkness by the highest navigational skill, aim their attacks, often under the heaviest fire, often with serious loss, with deliberate careful discrimination, and inflict shattering blows upon the whole of the technical and war-making structure of the Nazi power.

23

You are a small exclamation mark at the end of a very long and insignificant sentence in the book of history.

24

Take away that pudding – it has no theme.

25

I remember, when I was a child, being taken to the celebrated Barnum's circus, which contained an exhibition of freaks and monstrosities. But the exhibit on the programme which I most desired to see was the one described as "The Boneless Wonder." My parents judged that that spectacle would be too revolting and demoralising for my youthful eyes, and I have waited 50 years to see the boneless wonder sitting on the Treasury Bench.

26

The power of an air force is terrific when there is nothing to oppose it.

27

No one can guarantee success in war, but only deserve it.

28

Criticism may not be agreeable, but it is necessary. It fulfils the same function as pain in the human body. It calls attention to an unhealthy state of things.

29

The true characteristic of all British strategy lies in the use of amphibious power. Not the sea alone, but the land and the sea together: not the Fleet alone, but the Army in the hand of the Fleet.

30

In the twinkling of an eye I found myself without an office, without a seat, without a party, and without an appendix.

31

It is a mistake to try to look too far ahead. The chain of destiny can only be grasped one link at a time."

32

It was the nation and the race dwelling all round the globe that had the lion's heart. I had the luck to be called upon to give the roar.

33

Dictators ride to and fro on tigers from which they dare not dismount. And the tigers are getting hungry.

34

On Prime Minister Clement Attlee: There is less there than meets the eye.

35

A fanatic is one who can't change his mind and won't change the subject.

36

It has been said that democracy is the worst form of government except all the others that have been tried.

37

We have pushed taxation of wealth to a point in Great Britain where in many cases the yield would be greater if the rate were less. The idea that prosperity can be wooed by chasing millionaires is one of the most common and most foolish of modern popular delusions.

38

My most brilliant achievement was my ability to be able to persuade my wife to marry me.

39

Curse ruthless time! Curse our mortality. How cruelly short is the allotted span for all we must cram into it!

40

Uncounted generations will trample heedlessly upon our tombs. What is the use of living, if it be not to strive for noble causes and to make this muddled world a better place for those who will live in it after we are gone? How else can we put ourselves in harmonious relation with the great verities and consolations of the infinite and the eternal? And I avow my faith that we are marching towards better days. Humanity will not be cast down. We are going on swinging bravely forward along the grand high road and already behind the distant mountains is the promise of the sun.

41

I am fond of pigs. Dogs look up to us. Cats look down on us. Pigs treat us as equals.

42

We are masters of the unsaid words, but slaves of those we let slip out.

43

We contend that for a nation to try to tax itself into prosperity is like a man standing in a bucket and trying to lift himself up by the handle.

44

We are all worms. But I believe that I am a glow-worm.

45

Mr. Attlee is a very modest man. Indeed he has a lot to be modest about.

46

Uncounted generations will trample heedlessly upon our tombs. What is the use of living, if it be not to strive for noble causes and to make this muddled world a better place for those who will live in it after we are gone? How else can we put ourselves in harmonious relation with the great verities and consolations of the infinite and the eternal? And I avow my faith that we are marching towards better days. Humanity will not be cast down. We are going on swinging bravely forward along the grand high road and already behind the distant mountains is the promise of the sun.

47

I pass with relief from the tossing sea of Cause and Theory to the firm ground of Result and Fact.

48

I only believe in statistics that I doctored myself.

49

Fascism and Communism... Polar opposites—no, polar the same!

50

The heaviest cross I have to bear is the Cross of Lorraine.

51

A number of social problems arose. I had been told that neither smoking nor alcoholic beverages were allowed in the [Saudi] Royal Presence. As I was the host at luncheon I raised the matter at once, and said to the interpreter that if it was the religion of His Majesty [Ibn Saud] to deprive himself of smoking and alcohol I must point out that my rule of life prescribed as an absolutely sacred rite smoking cigars and also the drinking of alcohol before, after, and if need be during all meals and in the intervals between them. The King graciously accepted the position. His own cup-bearer from Mecca offered me a glass of water from its sacred well, the most delicious I had ever tasted.

52

First, Poland has been again overrun by two of the great powers which held her in bondage for 150 years but were unable to quench the spirit of the Polish nation. The heroic defence of Warsaw shows that the soul of Poland is indestructible, and that she will rise again like a rock which may for a spell be submerged by a tidal wave but which remains a rock.

53

The maxim Nothing avails but perfection may be spelt shorter: 'Paralysis.'

54

In War: Resolution. In Defeat: Defiance. In Victory: Magnanimity. In Peace: Good Will.

55

The story of the human race is war. Except for brief and precarious interludes, there has never been peace in the world; and before history began, murderous strife was universal and unending.

56

You have enemies? Good. That means you've stood up for something, sometime in your life.

57

If you're not a liberal when you're 25, you have no heart. If you're not a conservative by the time you're 35, you have no brain.

58

No idea is so outlandish that it should not be considered with a searching but at the same time a steady eye.

59

People often forget that in 1940 there was no guarantee that we were going to win.

60

Everyone can see how communism rots the soul of a nation. How it makes it abject in peace and proves it abominable in war.

61

When you are winning a war almost everything that happens can be claimed to be right and wise.

62

If you have ten thousand regulations you destroy all respect for the law.

63

Socialism is the philosophy of failure, the creed of ignorance and the gospel of envy.

64

It is a fine game to play - the game of politics - and it is well worth waiting for a good hand before really plunging.

65

It is not given to us to peer into the mysteries of the future. Still, I avow my hope and faith, sure and inviolate, that in the days to come the British and American peoples will for their own safety and for the good of all walk together side by side in majesty, in justice, and in peace.

66

You make a living by what you get; you make a life by what you give.

67

When we all got back to camp, our General communicated by heliograph through a distant mountain top with Sir Bindon Blood at Nawagai. Sir Bindon and our leading brigade had themselves been heavily attacked the night before. They had lost hundreds of animals and twenty or thirty men, but otherwise were none the worse. Sir Bindon sent orders that we were to stay in the Mamund valley and lay it waste with fire and sword in vengeance. This accordingly we did, but with great precautions. We proceeded systematically, village by village, and we destroyed the houses, filled up the wells, blew down the towers, cut down the great shady trees, burned the crops and broke the reservoirs in punitive devastation. So long as the villages were in the plain, this was quite easy. The tribesmen sat on the mountains and sullen watched the destruction of their homes and means of livelihood. When however we had to attack the villas on the sides of the mountains they resisted fiercely, and we lost for every village two or three British officers and fifteen or twenty native soldiers. Whether it was worth it, I cannot tell. At any rate, at the end of a fortnight the valley was a desert, and honour was satisfied.

68

We have surmounted all the perils and endured all the agonies of the past. We shall provide against and thus prevail over the dangers and problems of the future, withhold no sacrifice, grudge no toil, seek no sordid gain, fear no foe. All will be well. We have, I believe, within us the life-strength and guiding light by which the tormented world around us may find the harbour of safety, after a storm-beaten voyage.

69

Every morn brought forth a noble chance, and every chance brought forth a noble knight.

70

We make a living by what we get, but we make a life by what we give.

71

There are two things that are more difficult than making an after-dinner speech: climbing a wall which is leaning toward you and kissing a girl who is leaning away from you.

72

Lady Nancy Astor: If I were your wife I'd put poison in your coffee.
Churchill: If I were your husband I'd drink it.

73

I wonder whether any other generation has seen such astounding revolutions of data and values as those through which we have lived. Scarcely anything material or established which I was brought up to believe was permanent and vital, has lasted. Everything I was sure or taught to be sure was impossible, has happened.

74

Sure I am of this, that you have only to endure to conquer.

75

Everyone is in favour of free speech. Hardly a day passes without its being extolled, but some people's idea of it is that they are free to say what they like, but if anyone says anything back, that is an outrage

76

In finance, everything that is agreeable is unsound and everything that is sound is disagreeable."

77

India is a geographical term. It is no more a united nation than the Equator.

78

Baldwin thought Europe was a bore, and Chamberlain thought it was only a greater Birmingham.

79

Through our own folly and refusal to face realities and deal with evil tendencies while they were yet controllable, we have allowed brutal and intolerant forces to gain almost unchallenged supremacy in Europe and have placed ourselves in a position of weakness and peril, the like of which our history does not record for two and a half centuries.

80

I always seem to get inspiration and renewed vitality by contact with this great novel land of yours which sticks up out of the Atlantic.

81

Eaten bread is soon forgotten. Dangers which are warded off by effective precautions and foresight are never even remembered.

82

When I was younger I made it a rule never to take strong drink before lunch. It is now my rule never to do so before breakfast.

83

If you're going through hell, keep going.

84

Kites rise highest against the wind - not with it.

85

In the course of my life I have often had to eat my words, and I must confess that I have always found it a wholesome diet.

86

The whole history of the world is summed up in the fact that, when nations are strong, they are not always just, and when they wish to be just, they are no longer strong.

87

We shall draw from the heart of suffering itself the means of inspiration and survival.

88

Socialism is a philosophy of failure, the creed of ignorance, and the gospel of envy, its inherent virtue is the equal sharing of misery.

89

True genius resides in the capacity for evaluation of uncertain, hazardous, and conflicting information.

90

The long night of barbarism will descend, unbroken even by a star of hope, unless we conquer, as conquer we must; as conquer we shall.

91

History is written by the victors.

92

There is only one duty, only one safe course, and that is to try to be right and not to fear to do or say what you believe to be right.

93

I have never accepted what many people have kindly said, namely that I have inspired the nation. It was the nation and the race dwelling all around the globe that had the lion heart. I had the luck to be called upon to give the roar.

94

We know that he has, more than any other man, the gift of compressing the largest number of words into the smallest amount of thought.

95

Never hold discussions with the monkey when the organ grinder is in the room.

96

Jellicoe was the only man on either side who could lose the war in an afternoon.

97

When I am abroad, I always make it a rule never to criticize or attack the government of my own country. I make up for lost time when I come home.

98

If you go on with this nuclear arms race, all you are going to do is make the rubble bounce.

99

Historians are apt to judge war ministers less by the victories achieved under their direction than by the political results which flowed from them. Judged by that standard, I am not sure that I shall be held to have done very well.

100

We must beware of needless innovations, especially when guided by logic.

101

We shall show mercy, but we shall not ask for it.

102

A joke is a very serious thing.

103

Cultured people are merely the glittering scum which floats upon the deep river of production.

104

Play the game for more than you can afford to lose... only then will you learn the game.

105

Is this the end? Is it to be merely a chapter in a cruel and senseless story? Will a new generation in their turn be immolated to square the black accounts of the Teuton and Gaul? Will our children bleed and gasp again in devastated lands? Or will there spring from the very fires of conflict that reconciliation of the three giant combatants, which would unite their genius and secure to each in safety and freedom a share in rebuilding the glory of Europe.

106

Without tradition, art is a flock of sheep without a shepherd. Without innovation, it is a corpse.

107

I had a feeling once about Mathematics, that I saw it all—Depth beyond depth was revealed to me—the Byss and the Abyss. I saw, as one might see the transit of Venus—or even the Lord Mayor's Show, a quantity passing through infinity and changing its sign from plus to minus. I saw exactly how it happened and why the tergiversation was inevitable: and how the one step involved all the others. It was like politics. But it was after dinner and I let it go!

108

A free Press is the unsleeping guardian of every other right that freemen prize; it is the most dangerous foe of tyranny.

109

We are asking the nations of Europe between whom rivers of blood have flowed to forget the feuds of a thousand years.

110

I have taken more out of alcohol than alcohol has taken out of me.

111

Bessie Braddock: Winston, you are drunk, and what's more you are disgustingly drunk.

Churchill: Bessie, my dear, you are ugly, and, what's more, you are disgustingly ugly. But tomorrow I shall be sober and you will still be disgustingly ugly.

112

We do not covet anything from any nation except their respect.

113

Nothing can be more abhorrent to democracy than to imprison a person or keep him in prison because he is unpopular. This is really the test of civilization.

114

Although personally I am quite content with existing explosives, I feel we must not stand in the path of improvement.

115

The day may dawn when fair play, love for one's fellow men, respect for justice and freedom, will enable tormented generations to march forth triumphant from the hideous epoch in which we have to dwell. Meanwhile, never flinch, never weary, never despair.

116

For my own part I have always felt that a politician is to be judged by the animosities which he excites among his opponents. I have always set myself not merely to relish but to deserve thoroughly their censure.

117

It is always wise to look ahead, but difficult to look further than you can see.

118

Nothing in life is so exhilarating as to be shot at without result.

119

One does not leave a convivial party before closing time.

120

I like a man who grins when he fights.

121

We may now picture this great Fleet, with its flotillas and cruisers, steaming slowly out of Portland Harbour, squadron by squadron, scores of gigantic castles of steel wending their way across the misty, shining sea, like giants bowed in anxious thought. We may picture them again as darkness fell, eighteen miles of warships running at high speed and in absolute blackness through the narrow Straits, bearing with them into the broad waters of the North the safeguard of considerable affairs....The king's ships were at sea.

122

Someone once said that history is written by the victors. He probably was not the greatest of all victors, if only because his name has been utterly forgotten.

123

Governments create nothing and have nothing to give but what they have first taken away — you may put money in the pockets of one set of Englishmen, but it will be money taken from the pockets of another set of Englishmen, and the greater part will be spilled on the way. Every vote given for Protection is a vote to give Governments the right of robbing Peter to pay Paul and charging the public a handsome commission on the job.

124

In former days, when wars arose from individual causes, from the policy of a Minister or the passion of a King, when they were fought by small regular armies of professional soldiers, and when their course was retarded by the difficulties of communication and supply, and often suspended by the winter season, it was possible to limit the liabilities of the combatants. But now, when mighty populations are impelled on each other, each individual severally embittered and inflamed—when the resources of science and civilisation sweep away everything that might mitigate their fury, a European war can only end in the ruin of the vanquished and the scarcely less fatal commercial dislocation and exhaustion of the conquerors. Democracy is more vindictive than Cabinets. The wars of peoples will be more terrible than those of kings.

125

Defeat is one thing; disgrace is another.

126

If we open a quarrel between past and present, we shall find that we have lost the future.

127

The salvation of the common people of every race and of every land from war or servitude must be established on solid foundations and must be guarded by the readiness of all men and women to die rather than submit to tyranny.

128

One might as well legalise sodomy as recognise the Bolsheviks.

129

In war as in life, it is often necessary when some cherished scheme has failed, to take up the best alternative open, and if so, it is folly not to work for it with all your might.

130

If Hitler invaded Hell, I would make at least a favourable reference to the devil in the House of Commons.

131

Healthy citizens are the greatest asset any country can have.

132

Say what you have to say and the first time you come to a sentence with a grammatical ending – sit down.

133

I always avoid prophesying beforehand, because it is a much better policy to prophesy after the event has already taken place.

134

The reserve of modern assertions is sometimes pushed to extremes, in which the fear of being contradicted leads the writer to strip himself of almost all sense and meaning.

135

My wife and I tried two or three times in the last 40 years to have breakfast together, but it was so disagreeable we had to stop.

136

I could not write about the woe and ruin of the terrible twentieth century. We answered all the tests. But it was useless.

137

There is always much to be said for not attempting more than you can do and for making a certainty of what you try. But this principle, like others in life and war, has it exceptions.

138

The stations of uncensored expression are closing down; the lights are going out; but there is still time for those to whom freedom and parliamentary government mean something, to consult together. Let me, then, speak in truth and earnestness while time remains.

139

The wars fanned the wings of science, and science brought to mankind a thousand blessings, a thousand problems and a thousand perils.

140

The first duty of the university is to teach wisdom, not a trade; character, not technicalities. We want a lot of engineers in the modern world, but we do not want a world of engineers. "

141

Politics is the ability to foretell what is going to happen tomorrow, next week, next month and next year. And to have the ability afterwards to explain why it didn't happen.

142

It may be said, therefore, that the military opinion of the world is opposed to those people who cry 'Democratize the army!' and it must be remembered that an army is not a field upon which persons with Utopian ideas may exercise their political theories, but a weapon for the defence of the State.

143

Courage is rightly esteemed the first of human qualities... because it is the quality which guarantees all others.

144

I gather, young man, that you wish to be a Member of Parliament. The first lesson that you must learn is that, when I call for statistics about the rate of infant mortality, what I want is proof that fewer babies died when I was Prime Minister than when anyone else was Prime Minister. That is a political statistic.

145

Success is not final, failure is not fatal: it is the courage to continue that counts.

146

Broadly speaking, human beings may be divided into three classes: those who are toiled to death, those who are worried to death, and those who are bored to death.

147

It is more agreeable to have the power to give than to receive.

148

Difficulties mastered are opportunities won.

149

I'm just preparing my impromptu remarks.

150

Without a measureless and perpetual uncertainty, the drama of human life would be destroyed.

151

We shall defend our island, whatever the cost may be, we shall fight on the beaches, we shall fight on the landing grounds, we shall fight in the fields and in the streets, we shall fight in the hills; we shall never surrender.

152

I am certainly not one of those who need to be prodded. In fact, if anything, I am the prod.

153

There is no doubt that this is probably the greatest and most horrible crime ever committed in the whole history of the world, and it has been done by scientific machinery by nominally civilised men in the name of a great State and one of the leading races of Europe.

154

The very first thing the President did was to show me the new Presidential Seal, which he had just redesigned. He explained, 'The seal has to go everywhere the President goes. It must be displayed upon the lectern when he speaks. The eagle used to face the arrows but I have re-designed it so that it now faces the olive branches ... what do you think?' I said, 'Mr. President, with the greatest respect, I would prefer the American eagle's neck to be on a swivel so that it could face the olive branches or the arrows, as the occasion might demand.'

155

A pessimist sees the difficulty in every opportunity; an optimist sees the opportunity in every difficulty.

156

The only thing that ever really frightened me during the war was the U-boat peril.

157

Ending a sentence with a preposition is something up with which I will not put.

158

The mechanical danger must be overcome by a mechanical remedy.

159

This report, by its very length, defends itself against the risk of being read.

160

I do think unpunctuality is a vile habit, and all my life I have tried to break myself of it.

161

Do not let us speak of darker days; let us speak rather of sterner days. These are not dark days: these are great days – the greatest days our country has ever lived.

162

A love of tradition has never weakened a nation, indeed it has strengthened nations in their hour of peril; but the new view must come, the world must roll forward ... Let us have no fear of the future.

163

The empires of the future are the empires of the mind.

164

Many forms of Government have been tried and will be tried in this world of sin and woe. No one pretends that democracy is perfect or all-wise. Indeed, it has been said that democracy is the worst form of government except all those other forms that have been tried from time to time; but there is the broad feeling in our country that the people should rule, continuously rule, and that public opinion, expressed by all constitutional means, should shape, guide, and control the actions of Ministers who are their servants and not their masters.

165

Live dangerously; take things as they come; dread naught, all will be well.

166

The object of Parliament is to substitute argument for fisticuffs.

167

Courage is rightly esteemed the first of human qualities, because, as has been said, 'it is the quality which guarantees all others.'

168

The shores of History are strewn with the wrecks of Empires.

169

An empty taxi arrived and out of it stepped Attlee.

170

No compromise on the main purpose; no peace till victory; no pact with unrepentant wrong.

171

You see these dictators on their pedestals, surrounded by the bayonets of their soldiers and the truncheons of their police. On all sides they are guarded by masses of armed men, cannons, aeroplanes, fortifications, and the like — they boast and vaunt themselves before the world, yet in their hearts there is unspoken fear. They are afraid of words and thoughts; words spoken abroad, thoughts stirring at home — all the more powerful because forbidden — terrify them. A little mouse of thought appears in the room, and even the mightiest potentates are thrown into panic. They make frantic efforts to bar our thoughts and words; they are afraid of the workings of the human mind. Cannons, airplanes, they can manufacture in large quantities; but how are they to quell the natural promptings of human nature, which after all these centuries of trial and progress has inherited a whole armoury of potent and indestructible knowledge?

172

We live in a country where the people own the Government and not in a country where the Government owns the people. Thought is free, speech is free, religion is free, no one can say that the Press is not free. In short, we live in a liberal society, the direct product of the great advances in human dignity, stature and well-being which will ever be the glory of the nineteenth century.

173

In war, as in life, it is often necessary, when some cherished scheme has failed, to take up the best alternative open, and if so, it is folly not to work for it with all your might.

174

To jaw-jaw is always better than to war-war.

175

The stations of uncensored expression are closing down; the lights are going out; but there is still time for those to whom freedom and parliamentary government mean something, to consult together. Let me, then, speak in truth and earnestness while time remains.

176

I cannot pretend to be impartial about the colours. I rejoice with the brilliant ones, and am genuinely sorry for the poor browns.

177

It is a good thing for an uneducated man to read books of quotations.

178

I may be drunk, Miss, but in the morning I will be sober and you will still be ugly.

179

A prisoner of war is a man who tries to kill you and fails, and then asks you not to kill him.

180

Never, never, never believe any war will be smooth and easy, or that anyone who embarks on the strange voyage can measure the tides and hurricanes he will encounter. The statesman who yields to war fever must realise that once the signal is given, he is no longer the master of policy but the slave of unforeseeable and uncontrollable events. Antiquated War Offices, weak, incompetent, or arrogant Commanders, untrustworthy allies, hostile neutrals, malignant Fortune, ugly surprises, awful miscalculations — all take their seats at the Council Board on the morrow of a declaration of war. Always remember, however sure you are that you could easily win, that there would not be a war if the other man did not think he also had a chance.

181

The first quality that is needed is audacity.

182

On Golf: Like chasing a quinine pill around a cow pasture.

183

On Ramsay MacDonald: A sheep in sheep's clothing.

184

Every day you may make progress. Every step may be fruitful. Yet there will stretch out before you an ever-lengthening, ever-ascending, ever-improving path. You know you will never get to the end of the journey. But this, so far from discouraging, only adds to the joy and the glory of the climb.

185

One ought never to turn one's back on a threatened danger and try to run away from it. If you do that, you will double the danger. But if you meet it promptly and without flinching, you will reduce the danger by half. Never run away from anything. Never!

186

The era of procrastination, of half-measures, of soothing and baffling expedients, of delays, is coming to its close. In its place we are entering a period of consequences.

187

History will be kind to me for I intend to write it.

188

This is no war of chieftains or of princes, of dynasties or national ambition; it is a war of peoples and of causes. There are vast numbers, not only in this Island but in every land, who will render faithful service in this war, but whose names will never be known, whose deeds will never be recorded. This is a War of the Unknown Warrior; but let all strive without failing in faith or in duty, and the dark curse of Hitler will be lifted from our age.

189

We must all turn our backs upon the horrors of the past. We must look to the future. We cannot afford to drag forward cross the years that are to come the hatreds and revenges which have sprung from the injuries of the past.

190

The truth is incontrovertible. Malice may attack it, ignorance may deride it, but in the end, there it is.

191

The choice is between two ways of life: between individual liberty and State domination; between concentrations of ownership in the hands of the State and the extension of ownership over the widest number of individuals; between the dead hand of monopoly and the stimulus of competition; between a policy of increasing restraint and a policy of liberating energy and ingenuity; between a policy of leveling down and a policy of opportunity for all to rise upwards from a basic standard.

192

We shall not fail or falter. We shall not weaken or tire. Neither the sudden shock of battle nor the long-drawn trials of vigilance and exertion will wear us down. Give us the tools and we will finish the job.

193

The power of man has grown in every sphere, except over himself.

194

Men occasionally stumble over the truth, but most of them pick themselves up and hurry off as if nothing ever happened.

195

When we look back on all the perils through which we have passed and at the mighty foes that we have laid low and all the dark and deadly designs that we have frustrated, why should we fear for our future? We have come safely through the worst.

196

One ought never to turn one's back on a threatened danger and try to run away from it. If you do that, you will double the danger. But if you meet it promptly and without flinching, you will reduce the danger by half. Never run away from anything. Never!

197

What kind of a people do they think we are? Is it possible they do not realise that we shall never cease to persevere against them until they have been taught a lesson which they and the world will never forget?

198

I am easily satisfied with the very best.

199

Let our advance worrying become advance thinking and planning.

200

War arises from both sides feeling they have a hope of victory.

201

No part of the education of a politician is more indispensable than the fighting of elections.

202

If it weren't for painting, I wouldn't live; I couldn't bear the extra strain of things.

203

Do not let spacious plans for a new world divert your energies from saving what is left of the old.

204

I want no criticism of America at my table. The Americans criticize themselves more than enough.

205

Some people regard private enterprise as a predatory tiger to be shot. Others look on it as a cow they can milk. Not enough people see it as a healthy horse, pulling a sturdy wagon.

206

It is vain to recount further the catalogue of miseries. In earlier ages such horrors remain unknown because unrecorded. Just enough flickering light plays upon this infernal scene to give us the sense of its utter desolation and hopeless wretchedness and cruelty.

207

I cannot forecast to you the action of Russia. It is a riddle wrapped in a mystery inside an enigma.

208

I have no doubt that the Romans planned the time-table of their days far better than we do. They rose before the sun at all seasons. Except in wartime we never see the dawn. Sometimes we see sunset. The message of sunset is sadness; the message of dawn is hope. The rest and the spell of sleep in the middle of the day refresh the human frame far more than a long night. We were not made by Nature to work, or even play, from eight o'clock in the morning till midnight. We throw a strain upon our system which is unfair and improvident. For every purpose of business or pleasure, mental or physical, we ought to break our days and our marches into two.

209

I am always ready to learn although I do not always like being taught.

210

When the war of the giants is over the wars of the pygmies will begin.

211

What is adequacy? Adequacy is no standard at all."

212

Let us therefore brace ourselves to our duties, and so bear ourselves that, if the British Empire and its Commonwealth last for a thousand years, men will still say: "This was their finest hour."

213

I am never going to have anything more to do with politics or politicians. When this war is over I shall confine myself entirely to writing and painting.

214

It is a fine thing to be honest, but it is also very important to be right.

215

Certainly the prolonged education indispensable to the progress of Society is not natural to mankind. It cuts against the grain. A boy would like to follow his father in pursuit of food or prey. He would like to be doing serviceable things so far as his utmost strength allowed. He would like to be earning wages however small to help to keep up the home. He would like to have some leisure of his own to use or misuse as he pleased. He would ask little more than the right to work or starve. And then perhaps in the evenings a real love of learning would come to those who are worthy — and why try to stuff in those who are not? — and knowledge and thought would open the 'magic casements' of the mind.

216

They are afraid of words and thoughts; words spoken abroad, thoughts stirring at home — all the more powerful because forbidden — terrify them. A little mouse of thought appears in the room, and even the mightiest potentates are thrown into panic. They make frantic efforts to bar our thoughts and words; they are afraid of the workings of the human mind.

217

People say we ought not to allow ourselves to be drawn into a theoretical antagonism between Nazidom and democracy; but the antagonism is here now.

218

Where my reason, imagination or interest were not engaged, I would not or I could not learn.

219

The English never draw a line without blurring it.

220

There must be room in our army system for nearly everyone who is not grossly idle or grossly stupid. It is not a case of employing incompetent or worthless men, and such should, of course, be expelled from the army. It is a case of finding suitable employment for officers not fit for higher command.

221

The English know how to make the best of things. Their so-called muddling through is simply skill at dealing with the inevitable.

222

Every man should ask himself each day whether he is not too readily accepting negative solutions.

223

Don't talk to me about naval tradition. It's nothing but rum, sodomy, and the lash.

224

Where there is great power there is great responsibility, where there is less power there is less responsibility, and where there is no power there can, I think, be no responsibility.

225

I now began for the first time to envy those young cubs at the university who had fine scholars to tell them what was what; professors who had devoted their lives to mastering and focusing ideas in every branch of learning; who were eager to distribute the treasures they had gathered before they were overtaken by the night. But now I pity undergraduates, when I see what frivolous lives many of them lead in the midst of precious fleeting opportunity. After all, a man's Life must be nailed to a cross either of Thought or Action. Without work there is no play.

226

We have surmounted all the perils and endured all the agonies of the past. We shall provide against and thus prevail over the dangers and problems of the future, withhold no sacrifice, grudge no toil, seek no sordid gain, fear no foe. All will be well. We have, I believe, within us the life-strength and guiding light by which the tormented world around us may find the harbour of safety, after a storm-beaten voyage.

227

You are also mistaken in supposing that I have an anti-German obsession. British policy for four hundred years has been to oppose the strongest power in Europe by weaving together a combination of other countries strong enough to face the bully. Sometimes it is Spain, sometimes the French monarchy, sometimes the French Empire, sometimes Germany. I have no doubt who it is now...It is thus through the centuries we have kept our liberties and maintained our life and power.

228

I have been brought up and trained to have the utmost contempt for people who get drunk.

229

The price of greatness is responsibility.

230

The war between the Nazis and the Communists; the war of the non-God religions, waged with the weapons of the twentieth century. The most striking fact about the new religions was their similarity. They substituted the devil for God and hatred for love.

231

The reason for having diplomatic relations is not to confer a compliment, but to secure a convenience.

232

Politics is the ability to foretell what is going to happen tomorrow, next week, next month and next year. And to have the ability afterwards to explain why it didn't happen.

233

The power of the Executive to cast a man in prison without formulating any charge known to the law, and particularly to deny him the judgment of his peers is in the highest degree odious and is the foundation of all totalitarian government.

234

No crime is so great as daring to excel.

235

Too often the strong, silent man is silent only because he does not know what to say, and is reputed strong only because he has remained silent.

236

This is no time for ease and comfort. It is time to dare and endure.

237

Courage is what it takes to stand up and speak; courage is also what it takes to sit down and listen.

238

A lie gets halfway around the world before the truth has a chance to get its pants on.

239

Sure I am of this, that you have only to endure to conquer. You have only to persevere to save yourselves, and to save all those who rely upon you. You have only to go right on, and at the end of the road, be it short or long, victory and honor will be found.

240

We have not journeyed all this way across the centuries, across the oceans, across the mountains, across the prairies, because we are made of sugar candy.

241

The object of presenting medals, stars, and ribbons is to give pride and pleasure to those who have deserved them. At the same time a distinction is something which everybody does not possess. If all have it it is of less value ... A medal glitters, but it also casts a shadow.

242

I have never developed indigestion from eating my words.

243

How many wars have been precipitated by firebrands! How many misunderstandings which led to wars could have been removed by temporizing! How often have countries fought cruel wars and then after a few years found themselves not only friends but allies!

244

The inherent vice of capitalism is the unequal sharing of blessings; the inherent virtue of socialism is the equal sharing of miseries.

245

How many wars have been averted by patience and persisting good will!

246

From Stettin in the Baltic to Trieste in the Adriatic, an iron curtain has descended across the Continent.

247

We shape our buildings; thereafter they shape us.

248

It will not benefit the world if we succeed in banishing the old-fashioned wars of nations only to clear the board for social and doctrinal wars of even greater ferocity and destructiveness. This, indeed, is a growing danger. We were told that the old wars of religion had ended, but that is not much comfort if the wars of various kinds of secular religions or non-God religions are to begin and are to make Europe the arena of their hideous conflict, and if all that makes life worth living to the mass of the people is to be destroyed in the process.

249

We in this country, as in other Liberal and democratic countries, have a perfect right to exalt the principle of self-determination, but it comes ill out of the mouths of those in totalitarian States who deny even the smallest element of toleration to every section and creed within their bounds.

250

Study history, study history. In history lies all the secrets of statecraft.

251

This is only the beginning of the reckoning. This is only the first sip, the first foretaste of a bitter cup which will be proffered to us year by year unless by a supreme recovery of moral health and martial vigour, we arise again and take our stand for freedom as in the olden time.

252

I have not become the King's First Minister in order to preside over the liquidation of the British Empire.

253

Is there any need for further floods of agony? Is the only lesson of history to be that mankind is unteachable? Let there be justice, mercy and freedom. The people have only to will it, and all will achieve their hearts' desire.

254

Men who take up arms against the State must expect at any moment to be fired upon. Men who take up arms unlawfully cannot expect that the troops will wait until they are quite ready to begin the conflict.

255

When I make a statement of facts within my knowledge I expect it to be accepted.

256

The choice is between two ways of life: between individual liberty and State domination; between concentrations of ownership in the hands of the State and the extension of ownership over the widest number of individuals; between the dead hand of monopoly and the stimulus of competition; between a policy of increasing restraint and a policy of liberating energy and ingenuity; between a policy of leveling down and a policy of opportunity for all to rise upwards from a basic standard.

257

The fascists of the future will be called anti-fascists.

258

He has all of the virtues I dislike and none of the vices I admire.

259

if you will not fight for the right when you can easily win without bloodshed; if you will not fight when your victory will be sure and not too costly; you may come to the moment when you will have to fight with all the odds against you and only a precarious chance of survival. There may even be a worse case. You may have to fight when there is no hope of victory, because it is better to perish than to live as slaves.

260

There is no time for ease and comfort. It is time to dare and endure.

261

However beautiful the strategy, you should occasionally look at the results

262

Let me have the best solution worked out. Don't argue the matter. The difficulties will argue for themselves.

263

No hour of life is lost that is spent in the saddle.

264

We are stripped bare by the curse of plenty.

265

In those days he was wiser than he is now; he used to frequently take my advice.

266

I accumulated in those years so fine a surplus in the Book of Observance that I have been drawing confidently upon it ever since.

267

There are a terrible lot of lies going about the world, and the worst of it is that half of them are true.

268

We must recognise that we have a great treasure to guard; that the inheritance in our possession represents the prolonged achievement of the centuries; that there is not one of our simple uncounted rights today for which better men than we are have not died on the scaffold or the battlefield. We have not only a great treasure; we have a great cause. Are we taking every measure within our power to defend that cause?

269

The Times is speechless, and takes three columns to express its speechlessness.

270

Be the ordeal sharp or long, or both, we shall seek no terms, we shall tolerate no parley; we may show mercy—we shall ask for none.

271

The Balkans produce more history than they can consume.

272

To build may have to be the slow and laborious task of years. To destroy can be the thoughtless act of a single day.

273

All this contains much that is obviously true, and much that is relevant; unfortunately, what is obviously true is not relevant, and what is relevant is not obviously true.

274

We have differed and quarrelled in the past but now one bond unites us all—to wage war until victory is won, and never to surrender ourselves to servitude and shame, whatever the cost and the agony must be.

275

The problems of victory are more agreeable than those of defeat, but they are no less difficult.

276

Never in the field of human conflict was so much owed by so many to so few.

277

If this long island story of ours is to end at last, let it end only when each one of us lies choking in his own blood upon the ground.

278

Nicholas Soames: "Is it true, grandpapa, that you are the greatest man in the world?"
Churchill: "Yes I am. Now bugger off."

279

There is always a strong case for doing nothing, especially for doing nothing yourself.

280

If Hitler invaded hell I would make at least a favourable reference to the devil in the House of Commons.

281

I am an optimist. It does not seem too much use being anything else.

282

I have left the obvious, essential fact till this point, namely, that it is the Russian Armies who have done the main work in tearing the guts out of the German army. In the air and on the oceans we could maintain our place, but there was no force in the world which could have been called into being, except after several more years, that would have been able to maul and break the German army unless it had been subjected to the terrible slaughter and manhandling that has fallen to it through the strength of the Russian Soviet Armies.

283

Attitude is a little thing that makes a big difference.

284

Success is never found. Failure is never fatal. Courage is the only thing."

285

In war, you can only be killed once, but in politics, many times.

286

Those who can win a war well can rarely make a good peace, and those who could make a good peace would never have won the war.

287

Courage is rightly esteemed the first of human qualities because it has been said, it is the quality which guarantees all others.

288

Politics are very much like war. We may even have to use poison gas at times.

289

If the Almighty were to rebuild the world and asked me for advice, I would have English Channels round every country. And the atmosphere would be such that anything which attempted to fly would be set on fire.

290

These cruel, wanton, indiscriminate bombings of London are, of course, a part of Hitler's invasion plans. He hopes, by killing large numbers of civilians, and women and children, that he will terrorise and cow the people of this mighty imperial city ... Little does he know the spirit of the British nation, or the tough fibre of the Londoners.

291

Solitary trees, if they grow at all, grow strong.

292

Silly people, and there are many, not only in enemy countries, might discount the force of the United States. Some said they were soft, others that they would never be united. They would fool around at a distance. They would never come to grips. They would never stand bloodletting. Their democracy and system of recurrent elections would paralyse their war horizon to friend or foe. Now we should see the weakness of this numerous but remote, wealthy, and talkative people. But I had studied the American Civil War, fought out to the last desperate inch.

293

But we have our own dream and our own task. We are with Europe, but not of it. We are linked, but not comprised. We are interested and associated, but not absorbed.

294

Gentlemen, We Have Run Out Of Money; Now We Have to Think

295

Mr. Gladstone read Homer for fun, which I thought served him right.

296

We live in a country where the people own the Government and not in a country where the Government owns the people. Thought is free, speech is free, religion is free, no one can say that the Press is not free. In short, we live in a liberal society, the direct product of the great advances in human dignity, stature and well-being which will ever be the glory of the nineteenth century.

297

Democracy means that if the doorbell rings in the early hours, it is likely to be the milkman.

298

You can always count on Americans to do the right thing - after they've tried everything else.

299

If one has to submit, it is wasteful not to do so with the best grace possible.

300

The best argument against democracy is a five-minute conversation with the average voter.

301

Success consists of going from failure to failure without loss of enthusiasm.

302

The doctrines that by keeping out foreign goods more wealth, and consequently more employment, will be created at home, are either true or they are not true. We contend that they are not true. We contend that for a nation to try to tax itself into prosperity is like a man standing in a bucket and trying to lift himself up by the handle.[1]:9

303

When the eagles are silent, the parrots begin to jabber.

304

I have nothing to offer but blood, toil, tears and sweat.

305

And now go and set Europe ablaze...

306

We shall not fail or falter; we shall not weaken or tire. Neither the sudden shock of battle, nor the long-drawn trials of vigilance and exertion will wear us down. Give us the tools and we will finish the job.

307

Come on now all you young men, all over the world. You are needed more than ever now to fill the gap of a generation shorn by the war. You have not an hour to lose. You must take your places in Life's fighting line. Twenty to twenty-five! These are the years! Don't be content with things as they are. 'The earth is yours and the fulness thereof.' Enter upon your inheritance, accept your responsibilities. Raise the glorious flags again, advance them upon the new enemies, who constantly gather upon the front of the human army, and have only to be assaulted to be overthrown. Don't take No for an answer. Never submit to failure. Do not be fobbed off with mere personal success or acceptance. You will make all kinds of mistakes; but as long as you are generous and true, and also fierce, you cannot hurt the world or even seriously distress her.

308

Employ your time in improving yourself by other men's writings so that you shall come easily by what others have labored hard for.

309

Germany will recover and Russian will rise... our policy must be directed to prevent a union between German militarism and Russian Bolshevism.

310

You may try to destroy wealth, and find that all you have done is to increase poverty.

311

All the great things are simple, and many can be expressed in a single word: freedom, justice, honor, duty, mercy, hope.

312

There is no such thing as a good tax.

313

Great and good are seldom the same man.

314

The traditional British view is that character is what matters in a general. They like a solid, simple man, with no newfangled nonsense about him. He should be preternaturally silent. If by chance he thinks at all he should not let this leak out, otherwise confidence would be destroyed.

315

And now go and set Europe ablaze.

316

It is wonderful what great strides can be made when there is a resolute purpose behind them.

317

Anyone can rat, but it takes a certain amount of ingenuity to re-rat.

318

For my part, I consider that it will be found much better by all parties to leave the past to history, especially as I propose to write that history myself.

319

Hence, we will not say that Greeks fight like heroes, but that heroes fight like Greeks.

320

I was only the servant of my country and had I, at any moment, failed to express her unflinching resolve to fight and conquer, I should at once have been rightly cast aside.

321

It is no use saying, 'We are doing our best.' You have got to succeed in doing what is necessary.

322

The world looks with some awe upon a man who appears unconcernedly indifferent to home, money, comfort, rank, or even power and fame. The world feels not without a certain apprehension, that here is some one outside its jurisdiction; someone before whom its allurements may be spread in vain; some one strangely enfranchised, untamed, untrammelled by convention, moving independent of the ordinary currents of human action.

323

An appeaser is one who feeds a crocodile, hoping it will eat him last.

324

I hate nobody except Hitler — and that is professional.

325

We have always found the Irish a bit odd. They refuse to be English.

326

The great defense against the air menace is to attack the enemy's aircraft as near as possible to their point of departure.

327

Nothing can save England, if she will not save herself. If we lose faith in ourselves, in our capacity to guide and govern, if we lose our will to live, then, indeed, our story is told. If, while on all sides foreign nations are every day asserting a more aggressive and militant nationalism by arms and trade – if we remain paralysed by our own theoretical doctrines or plunged in the stupor of after-war exhaustion...indeed, all that the croakers predict will come true and our ruin will be certain and final.

328

Never, never, never believe any war will be smooth and easy, or that anyone who embarks on the strange voyage can measure the tides and hurricanes he will encounter. The statesman who yields to war fever must realize that once the signal is given, he is no longer the master of policy but the slave of unforeseeable and uncontrollable events.

329

For good or for ill, air mastery is today the supreme expression of military power and fleets and armies, however vital and important, must accept a subordinate rank.

330

Everything is overshadowed by the impending trial of will-power which is developing in Europe. I think we shall have to choose in the next few weeks between war and shame, and I have very little doubt what the decision will be.

331

Now this is not the end. It is not even the beginning of the end. But it is, perhaps, the end of the beginning.

332

Meeting Franklin Roosevelt was like opening your first bottle of champagne; knowing him was like drinking it.

333

Before Alamein we never had a victory. After Alamein we never had a defeat.

334

Everyone has his day, and some days last longer than others.

335

Really I feel less keen about the Army every day. I think the Church would suit me better.

336

Writing a book is an adventure. To begin with it is a toy then an amusement. Then it becomes a mistress, and then it becomes a master, and then it becomes a tyrant and, in the last stage, just as you are about to be reconciled to your servitude, you kill the monster and fling him to the public."

337

Battles are won by slaughter and maneuver. The greater the general, the more he contributes in maneuver, the less he demands in slaughter.

338

Although prepared for martyrdom, I preferred that it be postponed.

339

Continuous effort — not strength or intelligence — is the key to unlocking our potential.

340

To improve is to change; to be perfect is to change often.

341

The idea that a nation can tax itself into prosperity is one of the cruelest delusions which has befuddled the human mind.

342

You do your worst! — and we will do our best!

343

War is horrible, but slavery is worse, and you may be sure that the British people would rather go down fighting than live in servitude.

344

War is a game that is played with a smile. If you can't smile, grin. If you can't grin, keep out of the way till you can.

345

Broadly speaking short words are best and the old words when short, are best of all.

346

I don't like standing near the edge of a platform when an express train is passing through. I like to stand right back and if possible to get a pillar between me and the train. I don't like to stand by the side of a ship and look down into the water. A second's action would end everything. A few drops of desperation.

347

It is with deep grief I watch the clattering down of the British Empire, with all its glories and all the services it has rendered to mankind. ... Many have defended Britain against her foes. None can defend her against herself.

348

It is better to be making the news than taking it; to be an actor rather than a critic.

349

Frightfulness is not a remedy known to the British Pharmacopaeia.

350

In wartime, truth is so precious that she should always be attended by a bodyguard of lies.

351

I felt as if I were walking with destiny, and that all my past life had been but a preparation for this hour and for this trial.

352

Lenin was sent into Russia by the Germans in the same way that you might send a phial containing a culture of typhoid or cholera to be poured into the water supply of a great city, and it worked with amazing accuracy.

353

Time after time, history ran over the luddites and romanticists, those who sought to restore the old and delay the new. And every time, history did it with faster, more reliable and more advanced vehicles.

354

Taxes are an evil—a necessary evil, but still an evil, and the fewer of them we have the better.

355

When losses are made, under the present system those losses are borne by the individuals who sustained them and took the risk and judged things wrongly, whereas under State management all losses are quartered upon the taxpayers and the community as a whole. The elimination of the profit motive and of self-interest as a practical guide in the myriad transactions of daily life will restrict, paralyse and destroy British ingenuity, thrift, contrivance and good housekeeping at every stage in our life and production, and will reduce all our industries from a profit-making to a loss-making process.

356

If you have an important point to make, don't try to be subtle or clever. Use a pile driver. Hit the point once. Then come back and hit it again. Then hit it a third time - a tremendous whack.

357

My rule of life prescribed as an absolutely sacred rite smoking cigars and also the drinking of alcohol before, after and if need be during all meals and in the intervals between them.

358

Plans are of little importance, but planning is essential.

359

Every day you may make progress. Every step may be fruitful. Yet there will stretch out before you an ever-lengthening, ever-ascending, ever-improving path. You know you will never get to the end of the journey. But this, so far from discouraging, only adds to the joy and glory of the climb.

360

Never, never, never give up.

361

Bartlett's Familiar Quotations is an admirable work, and I studied it intently. The quotations when engraved upon the memory give you good thoughts. They also make you anxious to read the authors and look for more.

362

I am a sporting man. I always give them a fair chance to get away.

363

I have to come to think myself in the last lap of life that one should always look back upon the history of the past, study it and meditate upon it. Thus one learns the main line of advance...it is wrong to be bound by the events and commitments of the last few years, unless these are sound and compatible with the main historic line. I am sure the right course is to know as much as possible about all that has happened in the world, and then to act entirely upon the merits from day to day. Of course, my ideal is narrow and limited. I want to see the British Empire preserved for a few more generations in its strength and splendour. Only the most prodigious exertions of British genius will achieve this result.

364

We may indeed ask ourselves how it is that capitalism and free enterprise enable the United States not only to support its vast and varied life and needs, but also to supply these enormous sums to lighten the burden of others in distress.

365

There is no such thing as public opinion. There is only published opinion.

We hope that you have enjoyed this book.

For more editions just like this please search 'Abstract Press'.

ABSTRACT PRESS